WHY CHEMISTRY MATTERS

ELEMENTS AND COMPOUNDS

LYNNETTE BRENT

Crabtree Publishing Company

www.crabtreebooks.com

Crabtree Publishing Company

www.crabtreebooks.com

Author: Lynnette Brent
Coordinating editor: Chester Fisher
Series editor: Scholastic Ventures
Project manager: Santosh Vasudevan (Q2AMEDIA)
Art direction: Dibakar Acharjee (Q2AMEDIA)
Cover design: Ranjan Singh (Q2AMEDIA)
Design: Tarang Saggar (Q2AMEDIA)
Photo research: Sejal Sehgal Wani (Q2AMEDIA)
Editor: Adrianna Morganelli
Proofreader: Crystal Sikkens
Project editor: Robert Walker
Production coordinator: Katherine Kantor
Font management: Mike Golka
Prepress technicians:
Margaret Amy Salter, Ken Wright, Katherine Kantor

Photographs:
Cover: Pinfoldphotos/Dreamstime (background), Alex Kosev/ Shutterstock (coins), Sweetym/Istockphoto (gold bars); Title page: Andrey Kiselev/Russian Federation/123RF; P4: Claudio Divizia/ Shutterstock (top left); P4: Sílvia Antunes/Shutterstock (top right); P4: Brasiliao-media/Shutterstock (center); P4: Djpj/BigStockPhoto (bottom); P5: Rich Legg/Istockphoto; P6: Ljupco Smokovski/ Shutterstock; P8: Orla/Shutterstock; P9: Williv/Istockphoto; P10: NASA; P11: NASA; P12: Donkompot/Dreamstime; P13: S-dmit/Dreamstime (bottom); P14: Philip Lange/Shutterstock; P16: YouraPechkin/Shutterstock; P17: Baka/BigStockPhoto (top left); P17: Sprinter81/Shutterstock (bottom right); P18: Steven HeapPress/ Shutterstock; P19: Emin Kuliyev/Shutterstock (bottom); P21: Jim West/Alamy; P23: Pederk/Istockphoto (bottom left); P23: Mediablitzimages (UK) Limited/ Alamy (bottom center); P23: Difydave/Istockphoto (bottom right); P25: Konstantins Visnevskis/Shutterstock (bottom); P26: Dndavis/BigStockPhoto; P27: Wendell Franks/Istockphoto (top); P27: P Barber – CMSP/Getty Images (bottom); P28: Anne Kitzman/Shutterstock; P29: Pidjoe/ Istockphoto (top); P29: Comstock Images/Jupiter Images (bottom)

Illustrations:
Q2A Media Art Bank: P 5, 7, 13 (top), 15, 17 (top right and bottom left), 19 (top), 20, 22, 24, 25 (top)

Library and Archives Canada Cataloguing in Publication

Brent, Lynnette, 1974-
 Elements and compounds / Lynnette Brent.

(Why chemistry matters)
Includes index.
ISBN 978-0-7787-4242-5 (bound).--ISBN 978-0-7787-4249-4 (pbk.)

1. Chemical elements--Juvenile literature. 2. Organic compounds--

Juvenile literature. 3. Chemistry--Juvenile literature. I. Title. II. Series.

QD466.W43 2008   j546   C2008-904139-9

Library of Congress Cataloging-in-Publication Data

Brent, Lynnette, 1974-
 Elements and compounds / Lynnette Brent.
  p. cm. -- (Why chemistry matters)
 Includes index.
 ISBN-13: 978-0-7787-4249-4 (pbk. : alk. paper)
 ISBN-10: 0-7787-4249-0 (pbk. : alk. paper)
 ISBN-13: 978-0-7787-4242-5 (reinforced library binding : alk. paper)
 ISBN-10: 0-7787-4242-3 (reinforced library binding : alk. paper)
 1. Chemical elements--Juvenile literature. 2. Organic compounds--Juvenile
literature. 3. Chemstry--Juvenile literature. I. Title. II. Series.

QD466.B636 2009
546--dc22

                              2008028895

Crabtree Publishing Company

www.crabtreebooks.com   1-800-387-7650

Published in Canada
Crabtree Publishing
616 Welland Ave.
St. Catharines, ON
L2M 5V6

Published in the United States
Crabtree Publishing
PMB16A
350 Fifth Ave., Suite 3308
New York, NY 10118

Published in the United Kingdom
Crabtree Publishing
White Cross Mills
High Town, Lancaster
LA1 4XS

Published in Australia
Crabtree Publishing
386 Mt. Alexander Rd.
Ascot Vale (Melbourne)
VIC 3032

Contents

Elements

Today we know so much about the world around us, it might be hard to believe that long ago humans had no idea what made up their surroundings. What mysterious substances made up rocks, plants, animals, and people? More than 2,300 years ago, a Greek philosopher named Aristotle (ae-rih-**sta**-tel) tried to answer these questions. He suggested that everything in the universe was made of four basic building blocks: earth, air, fire, and water.

This idea was popular until the 1600s. Around that time, scientists began to discover the true **elements**. Elements are substances, such as oxygen and gold, that cannot be split into simpler substances. Gold, for instance, is often found combined with other rocks in a mixture called **ore**. People can use heat to separate gold from the other rocks. The gold, though, stays just as it is. It is an element.

By 1869, scientists had discovered 63 elements. That year, a scientist named Dmitri Mendeleyev (dih-**me**-tree men-del-**ay**-ev) arranged those elements by classifying them into groups. Many groups of elements have special names, like **alkali metals** or **noble gases**. You will learn more about the groups later in this book.

Mendeleyev's grouping of elements was the first **periodic table**. In the years since, scientists have discovered dozens more elements, some easy to find and some very rare. Today, the periodic table of the elements contains 117 elements.

The Greek philosopher Aristotle believed the universe was made of four elements--earth, air, fire, and water.

Scientists are still discovering new elements. The two most recent were discovered in a lab in Russia in 2004.

Atoms and Elements

*Elements are substances made of particles called **atoms**. Elements contain only one type of atom. The element hydrogen contains only hydrogen atoms. The element oxygen contains only oxygen atoms. Atoms can join to form larger particles called **molecules**. Water is a molecule made of hydrogen and oxygen atoms. Water has two types of atoms, so it is not an element.*

The Periodic Table

The periodic table is a chart of the elements. You will notice it is a grid. The elements are placed in the periodic table because of how they look and act.

At their centers, atoms have a core called a **nucleus**. The nucleus has tiny particles called **protons** and **neutrons** inside it. Have you ever seen the + and the – on a battery? Those are electrical charges. Protons are particles with positive charges. Neutrons are particles without any charge. Each atom also has particles called **electrons**. Electrons have a negative charge. Electrons circle around the atom's nucleus. Think of a planet orbiting the Sun, and you have a picture of electrons circling the nucleus of an atom.

Every element has a different number of protons in its atoms. The number of protons in an atom is the **atomic number**. That number is the same as the number of electrons moving around the nucleus. Hydrogen has the atomic number 1. That means every hydrogen atom has one proton and one electron. Helium's atomic number is 2. What does that mean about the atoms in helium? It means that a helium atom always has two protons and two electrons.

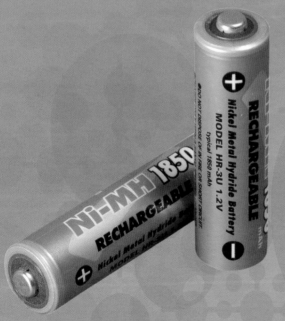

The + and - on the battery indicate positive and negative charge, just like protons (+) and electrons (-) in an atom.

Periodic Prediction

When Mendeleyev arranged the elements in the periodic table, he lined them up according to their atomic numbers. At the time, many of the elements had not been found yet. Mendeleyev predicted the elements would be found and left blank spots for them on his table. When scientists found these elements, they fit in where Mendeleyev said they would.

Periodic Table of Elements

Key

relative atomic mass
atomic number
name
atomic (proton) number

Example:

1.0
H
hydrogen
1

(1)	(2)		(3)	(4)	(5)	(6)	(7)	(8)	(9)	(10)	(11)	(12)	(13)	(14)	(15)	(16)	(17)	(18)
																		4.0 **He** helium 2
6.9 **Li** lithium 3	9.0 **Be** beryllium 4												10.8 **B** boron 5	12.0 **C** carbon 6	14.0 **N** nitrogen 7	16.0 **O** oxygen 8	19.0 **F** fluorine 9	20.2 **Ne** neon 10
23.0 **Na** sodium 11	24.3 **Mg** magnesium 12												27.0 **Al** aluminium 13	28.1 **Si** silicon 14	31.0 **P** phosphorus 15	32.1 **S** sulphur 16	35.5 **Cl** chlorine 17	39.9 **Ar** argon 18
39.1 **K** potassium 19	40.1 **Ca** calcium 20		45.0 **Sc** scandium 21	47.9 **Ti** titanium 22	50.9 **V** vanadium 23	52.0 **Cr** chromium 24	54.9 **Mn** manganese 25	55.8 **Fe** iron 26	58.9 **Co** cobalt 27	58.7 **Ni** nickel 28	63.5 **Cu** copper 29	65.4 **Zn** zinc 30	69.7 **Ga** gallium 31	72.6 **Ge** germanium 32	74.9 **As** arsenic 33	79.0 **Se** selenium 34	79.9 **Br** bromine 35	83.8 **Kr** krypton 36
85.5 **Rb** rubidium 37	87.6 **Sr** strontium 38		88.9 **Y** yttrium 39	91.2 **Zr** zirconium 40	92.9 **Nb** niobium 41	95.9 **Mo** molybdenum 42	98.9 **Tc** technetium 43	101.1 **Ru** ruthenium 44	102.9 **Rh** rhodium 45	106.4 **Pd** palladium 46	107.9 **Ag** silver 47	112.4 **Cd** cadmium 48	114.8 **In** indium 49	118.7 **Sn** tin 50	121.8 **Sb** antimony 51	127.6 **Te** tellurium 52	126.9 **I** iodine 53	131.3 **Xe** xenon 54
132.9 **Cs** caesium 55	137.3 **Ba** barium 56		138.9 **La *** lanthanum 57	178.5 **Hf** hafnium 72	180.9 **Ta** tantalum 73	183.9 **W** tungsten 74	186.2 **Re** rhenium 75	190.2 **Os** osmium 76	192.2 **Ir** iridium 77	195.1 **Pt** platinum 78	197.0 **Au** gold 79	200.6 **Hg** mercury 80	204.4 **Tl** thallium 81	207.2 **Pb** lead 82	209.0 **Bi** bismuth 83	210.0 **Po** polonium 84	210.0 **At** astatine 85	222.0 **Rn** radon 86
[223.0] **Fr** francium 87	[226.0] **Ra** radium 88		[227] **Ac †** actinium 89	[261] **Rf** rutherfordium 104	[262] **Db** dubnium 105	[266] **Sg** seaborgium 106	[264] **Bh** bohnium 107	[277] **Hs** hassium 108	[268] **Mt** meitnerium 109	[271] **Ds** darmstadium 110	[272] **Rg** roentgenium 111							

Elements with atomic numbers 112-116 have been reported but not fully authenticad

* 58 – 71 Lanthanides

140.1 **Ce** cerium 58	140.9 **Pr** praseodymium 59	144.2 **Nd** neodymium 60	144.9 **Pm** promethium 61	150.4 **Sm** samarium 62	152.0 **Eu** europium 63	157.3 **Gd** gadolinium 64	158.9 **Tb** terbium 65	162.5 **Dy** dysprosium 66	164.9 **Ho** holmium 67	167.3 **Er** erbium 68	168.9 **Tm** thulium 69	173.0 **Yb** ytterbium 70	175.0 **Lu** lutetium 71

† 90 – 103 Actinides

232.0 **Th** thorium 90	231.0 **Pa** protactinium 91	238.0 **U** uranium 92	237.0 **Np** neptunium 93	239.1 **Pu** plutonium 94	243.1 **Am** americium 95	247.1 **Cm** curium 96	247.1 **Bk** berkelium 97	252.1 **Cf** californium 98	[252] **Es** einsteinium 99	[257] **Fm** fermium 100	[258] **Md** mendelevium 101	[259] **No** nobelium 102	[260] **Lr** lawrencium 103

Take a look at the periodic table. What do you notice about the elements' atomic numbers? Elements are arranged from left to right according to their atomic numbers.

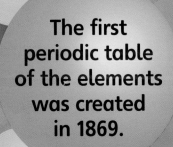

The first periodic table of the elements was created in 1869.

How did the period table get its name? Each of the rows is a different period. The columns are **groups**. Each group has the same number of electrons in its outer shell. Elements in each group often have other features in common. One group is made of elements that explode when mixed with water. Another group is made of all stinky, poisonous gases. The two elements at the top, hydrogen and helium, are special elements. Hydrogen could belong to two different groups. Helium can only have two electrons in its outer shell, but it acts like elements that have eight.

Each box on the periodic table shows the element's atomic number, the number of protons in the element's atoms. Each box also shows the element's name and **chemical symbol**. The chemical symbol is one or two letters. Most chemical symbols come from an element's English name. Some come from other languages. Mercury is a silver-colored element that is liquid at room temperature. Its symbol, *Hg*, comes from *hydrargyrum* (hy-**drahr**-jer-uhm), the old Greek word for "liquid silver." That word definitely describes mercury!

Many periodic tables also tell each element's **atomic mass**. The atomic mass is the total mass of one atom of the element. Atomic mass is measured in units called atomic mass units (amu). The atomic mass of the element carbon, for example, is 12 amu.

Atoms are made of three tiny particles: protons, electrons, and neutrons. The number of protons is the element's atomic number.

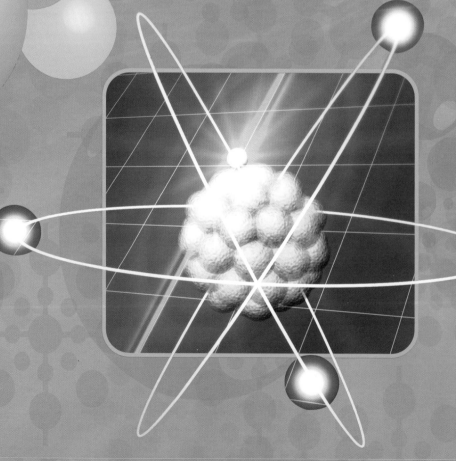

Understanding Isotopes

The number of protons and electrons inside an atom never changes, but the number of neutrons might. A carbon atom always has six protons and electrons. Usually, carbon has 12 neutrons, but it can have 14. Carbon with 14 neutrons is an **isotope** of carbon. An isotope is a form of an element with a different number of neutrons than usual.

The chemical symbol for iron is Fe (from the Latin ferrum). Iron helps us build things and keeps plants and animals alive.

Hydrogen

You already know that hydrogen holds the first spot on the periodic table, with the atomic number 1. So what makes hydrogen so special? Hydrogen has no color, no flavor, and no smell. Yet there is more hydrogen in the universe than any other element. It is estimated to make up more than 90 percent of all atoms. The Sun and many other stars are made mostly of hydrogen. Jupiter is made almost entirely of hydrogen. On Earth, hydrogen is usually found mixed together with other elements. Hydrogen links up with oxygen atoms to form water. Molecules made of hydrogen and carbon form the important building blocks of plant and animal tissues.

Stars like our Sun are super hot balls of gases. Our Sun is 70 percent hydrogen gas.

Hydrogen is very light. It weighs 1/10 as much as air. Pure hydrogen gas is very **flammable**—it catches fire easily and burns quickly. When cooled to -252.87 degrees Celsius (-423.17 Fahrenheit), hydrogen turns into a liquid. Liquid hydrogen is also flammable. It is often used as a fuel for rockets.

Hydrogen has many uses for businesses as well. Hydrogen is part of the process used to make plant food. Welders use hydrogen as part of their process of bonding metals together. Did you spread margarine on your toast this morning? Then you got a little dose of hydrogen! Hydrogen is added to liquid oils to make solid fats like margarine and shortening.

The Hindenburg airship was filled with hydrogen gas. It exploded when the flammable gas caught fire.

The Hindenburg Explosion

Hydrogen gas was once used to fill balloons and airships. In 1937, an airship called the Hindenburg burst into flames as it was landing in the United States. The ship was filled with hydrogen. The flammable gas quickly caught fire. Thirty-six people died. Today, most blimps are filled with helium instead, a lightweight gas that is not as flammable as hydrogen.

Metals

Some of the groups in the periodic table are known by special names. They are categorized because of properties they have that make them alike in some way. The two columns on the left side of the periodic table contain elements called the **alkali** (al-kuh-lahy) **metals** and the **alkaline** (al-kuh-lahyn) **earth metals**.

The alkali metals are very **reactive**. This means that they can mix very easily with water or other elements. When they mix, they often explode or give off harmful gases. Alkalis also burn easily in air. Alkali metals are not usually found in their pure forms. Instead, they are often found in **compounds**. Compounds are materials made of two or more different elements. The alkali metal sodium, for example, is not usually found by itself. Instead, it is commonly found stuck to the element chlorine in a compound called sodium chloride (NaCl). Sodium chloride is the chemical name for table salt. Table salt is very safe. Sodium by itself, however, is not.

The alkaline earth metals are similar to alkali metals. They are not quite as reactive, though. Alkaline earth metals can give off intense light and bright colors when they burn. Have you ever enjoyed the bright color and sparkle of fireworks? Many fireworks contain alkaline earth metals. Different alkaline earth metals create different colors in the fireworks.

Alkaline earth metals are ingredients that give the pop and sparkle to holiday firework displays.

Periodic Table of Elements

Key
relative atomic mass
atomic number
name
atomic (proton) number

(1)	(2)	(3)	(4)	(5)	(6)	(7)	(8)	(9)	(10)	(11)	(12)	(13)	(14)	(15)	(16)	(17)	(18)
						1.0 H hydrogen 1											4.0 He helium 2
6.9 Li lithium 3	9.0 Be beryllium 4											10.8 B boron 5	12.0 C carbon 6	14.0 N nitrogen 7	16.0 O oxygen 8	19.0 F fluorine 9	20.2 Ne neon 10
23.0 Na sodium 11	24.3 Mg magnesium 12											27.0 Al aluminium 13	28.1 Si silicon 14	31.0 P phosphorus 15	32.1 S sulphur 16	35.5 Cl chlorine 17	39.9 Ar argon 18
39.1 K potassium 19	40.1 Ca calcium 20	45.0 Sc scandium 21	47.9 Ti titanium 22	50.9 V vanadium 23	52.0 Cr chromium 24	54.9 Mn manganese 25	55.8 Fe iron 26	58.9 Co cobalt 27	58.7 Ni nickel 28	63.5 Cu copper 29	65.4 Zn zinc 30	69.7 Ga gallium 31	72.6 Ge germanium 32	74.9 As arsenic 33	79.0 Se selenium 34	79.9 Br bromine 35	83.8 Kr krypton 36
85.5 Rb rubidium 37	87.6 Sr strontium 38	88.9 Y yttrium 39	91.2 Zr zirconium 40	92.9 Nb niobium 41	95.9 Mo molybdenum 42	98.9 Tc technetium 43	101.1 Ru ruthenium 44	102.9 Rh rhodium 45	106.4 Pd palladium 46	107.9 Ag silver 47	112.4 Cd cadmium 48	114.8 In indium 49	118.7 Sn tin 50	121.8 Sb antimony 51	127.6 Te tellurium 52	126.9 I iodine 53	131.1 Xe xenon 54
132.9 Cs caesium 55	137.3 Ba barium 56	138.9 La* lanthanum 57	178.5 Hf hafnium 72	180.9 Ta tantalum 73	183.9 W tungsten 74	186.2 Re rhenium 75	190.2 Os osmium 76	192.2 Ir iridium 77	195.1 Pt platinum 78	197.0 Au gold 79	200.6 Hg mercury 80	204.4 Tl thallium 81	207.2 Pb lead 82	209.0 Bi bismuth 83	210.0 Po polonium 84	210.0 At astatine 85	222.0 Rn radon 86
[223.0] Fr francium 87	[226.0] Ra radium 88	[227] Ac† actinium 89	[261] Rf rutherfordium 104	[262] Db dubnium 105	[266] Sg seaborgium 106	[264] Bh bohnium 107	[277] Hs hassium 108	[268] Mt meitnerium 109	[271] Ds darmstadium 110	[272] Rg roentgenium 111							

Elements with atomic numbers 112-116 have been reported but not fully authenticad

* 58 – 71 Lanthanides

† 90 – 103 Actinides

140.1 Ce cerium 58	140.9 Pr praseodymium 59	144.2 Nd neodymium 60	144.9 Pm promethium 61	150.4 Sm samarium 62	152.0 Eu europium 63	157.3 Gd gadolinium 64	158.9 Tb terbium 65	162.5 Dy dysprosium 66	164.9 Ho holmium 67	167.3 Er erbium 68	168.9 Tm thulium 69	173.0 Yb ytterbium 70	175.0 Lu lutetium 71
232.0 Th thorium 90	231.0 Pa protactinium 91	238.0 U uranium 92	237.0 Np neptunium 93	239.1 Pu plutonium 94	243.1 Am americium 95	247.1 Cm curium 96	247.1 Bk berkelium 97	252.1 Cf californium 98	[252] Es einsteinium 99	[257] Fm fermium 100	[258] Md mendelevium 101	[259] No nobelium 102	[260] Lr lawrencium 103

Alkali metals (orange) and alkaline earth metals (purple) are grouped together on the left side of the periodic table.

Calcium and Human Health

Calcium is a soft, silvery-white alkali metal, the fifth most common element on the planet. It is found in chalk, limestone, and seashells. It is also important for life. Calcium is essential for teeth, bones, and healthy muscles. People who do not get enough calcium suffer from a disease called rickets, which causes weak bones.

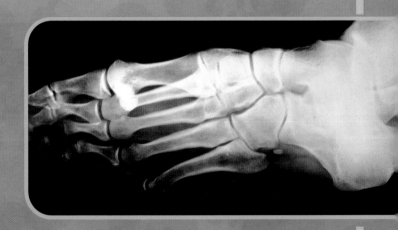

Calcium is an important part of human bones and teeth. Getting plenty of calcium in your diet can help prevent broken bones.

Moving along on the periodic table, the next group is the **transition elements**. The 59 transition elements are all **metals**. Metals are shiny elements that are usually strong and hard. (True metals are different from alkali metals and alkaline earth metals.) You are probably familiar with many of these elements, such as iron, nickel, copper, and gold. These metals have been important to humans for thousands of years. They knew how to create jewelry and weapons from copper. Two sets of transition elements are usually pictured on their own at the bottom of the periodic table. These elements are the **lanthanides** (**lan**-thuh-nahyds) and the **actinides** (**ak**-tuh-nahyd).

Radioactive!

*When radioactive elements lose particles from their atoms, they give off energy called **radiation**. Radiation is used to take X-ray pictures of peoples' bones. Radioactive elements can also be used for energy. Nuclear power plants convert radiation into electricity. Too much radiation can be dangerous. People who are around a lot of radiation can become sick or even die.*

Inside nuclear power plants, radioactive elements are used to create energy.

Periodic Table of Elements

Key

1.0
H
hydrogen
1

relative atomic mass
atomic number
name
atomic (proton) number

(1)	(2)		(3)	(4)	(5)	(6)	(7)	(8)	(9)	(10)	(11)	(12)	(13)	(14)	(15)	(16)	(17)	(18)
																		4.0 He helium 2
6.9 Li lithium 3	9.0 Be beryllium 4												10.8 B boron 5	12.0 C carbon 6	14.0 N nitrogen 7	16.0 O oxygen 8	19.0 F fluorine 9	20.2 Ne neon 10
23.0 Na sodium 11	24.3 Mg magnesium 12												27.0 Al aluminium 13	28.1 Si silicon 14	31.0 P phosphorus 15	32.1 S sulphur 16	35.5 Cl chlorine 17	39.9 Ar argon 18
39.1 K potassium 19	40.1 Ca calcium 20		45.0 Sc scandium 21	47.9 Ti titanium 22	50.9 V vanadium 23	52.0 Cr chromium 24	54.9 Mn manganese 25	55.8 Fe iron 26	58.9 Co cobalt 27	58.7 Ni nickel 28	63.5 Cu copper 29	65.4 Zn zinc 30	69.7 Ga gallium 31	72.6 Ge germanium 32	74.9 As arsenic 33	79.0 Se selenium 34	79.9 Br bromine 35	83.8 Kr krypton 36
85.5 Rb rubidium 37	87.6 Sr strontium 38		88.9 Y yttrium 39	91.2 Zr zirconium 40	92.9 Nb niobium 41	95.9 Mo molybdenum 42	98.9 Tc technetium 43	101.1 Ru ruthenium 44	102.9 Rh rhodium 45	106.4 Pd palladium 46	107.9 Ag silver 47	112.4 Cd cadmium 48	114.8 In indium 49	118.7 Sn tin 50	121.8 Sb antimony 51	127.6 Te tellurium 52	126.9 I iodine 53	131.3 Xe xenon 54
132.9 Cs caesium 55	137.3 Ba barium 56		138.9 La* lanthanum 57	178.5 Hf hafnium 72	180.9 Ta tantalum 73	183.9 W tungsten 74	186.2 Re rhenium 75	190.2 Os osmium 76	192.2 Ir iridium 77	195.1 Pt platinum 78	197.0 Au gold 79	200.6 Hg mercury 80	204.4 Tl thallium 81	207.2 Pb lead 82	209.0 Bi bismuth 83	210.0 Po polonium 84	210.0 At astatine 85	222.0 Rn radon 86
[223.0] Fr francium 87	[226.0] Ra radium 88		[227] Ac† actinium 89	[261] Rf rutherfordium 104	[262] Db dubnium 105	[266] Sg seaborgium 106	[264] Bh bohnium 107	[277] Hs hassium 108	[268] Mt meitnerium 109	[271] Ds darmstadium 110	[272] Rg roentgenium 111							

Elements with atomic numbers 112-116 have been reported but not fully authenticad

* 58 – 71 Lanthanides

140.1 Ce cerium 58	140.9 Pr praseodymium 59	144.2 Nd neodymium 60	144.9 Pm promethium 61	150.4 Sm samarium 62	152.0 Eu europium 63	157.3 Gd gadolinium 64	158.9 Tb terbium 65	162.5 Dy dysprosium 66	164.9 Ho holmium 67	167.3 Er erbium 68	168.9 Tm thulium 69	173.0 Yb ytterbium 70	175.0 Lu lutetium 71

† 90 – 103 Actinides

232.0 Th thorium 90	231.0 Pa protactinium 91	238.0 U uranium 92	237.0 Np neptunium 93	239.1 Pu plutonium 94	243.1 Am americium 95	247.1 Cm curium 96	247.1 Bk berkelium 97	252.1 Cf californium 98	[252] Es einsteinium 99	[257] Fm fermium 100	[258] Md mendelevium 101	[259] No nobelium 102	[260] Lr lawrencium 103

The lanthanides are rare, shiny elements. They have the atomic numbers 57 to 71. They are sometimes in compounds with other elements. Often, they are inside rare **minerals**. Minerals are solid compounds that are formed by Earth activities. They might have formed when a volcano erupted or when mountains were growing millions of years ago.

The actinides have the atomic numbers 89 to 103. They are **radioactive** elements. Radioactive elements are not very stable. Over time, they lose the particles in their atoms. When that happens, they change into different elements. The radioactive element uranium, for example, changes into the element lead. It does not happen quickly, though. The change takes billions of years!

The transition elements (dark blue) are metals that fill up the center of the periodic table.

Metals and Nonmetals

The next group on the periodic table is harder to classify. Some of the elements in the group are metals, like lead and tin. The metal aluminium is very common. There is a large amount of lightweight, silver-colored aluminium in the rocks of Earth's crust. Aluminium has many uses in our daily lives, from soda cans and kitchen utensils to gutters and signs. Sometimes aluminium is blended with other metals, like copper or zinc, to make a stronger metal. When different metals are blended together, the metal that is created is called an **alloy**.

Other elements in this group are called nonmetals. Oxygen and nitrogen, for example, are nonmetals. These elements are gases at room temperature. Oxygen and nitrogen are the two most common gases in the air we breathe. Other nonmetals in this group are also important to life. Carbon, for example, plays an important part in the structure of plant and animal cells.

Some of the elements in this part of the periodic table are even harder to describe. They are not exactly metals. Yet they are often similar to metals in certain ways. These elements are **metalloids**. Metalloids sometimes look shiny like metals. Usually they are not as hard and strong as true metals. One important metalloid is silicon (Si). Without silicon, your computer, cell phone, and MP3 player wouldn't exist!

Computer chips are made from the metalloid element silicon. Silicon may be hard to classify—but it is extremely useful!

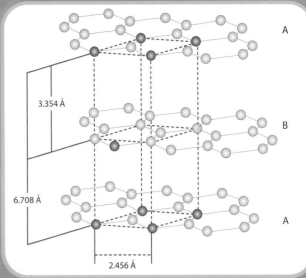

3.354 Å

6.708 Å

2.456 Å

A

B

A

You probably would not write with a diamond, but diamond gemstones and the graphite in pencils are both forms of carbon.

Carbon's Many Faces

The lead in your pencil is made from a soft, black material called graphite. Diamonds, on the other hand, are crystal clear and very hard. Graphite and diamonds seem very different. In fact, they are both made only from the element carbon! Atoms of carbon can come together in different ways to form very different materials.

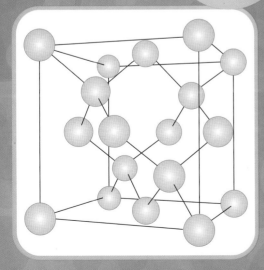

Halogens and Noble Gases

Opposite from the alkali and alkaline earth metals, on the far right of the periodic table, are the **halogens** and noble gases. The halogen group begins with the element fluorine (**flohr**-een). The noble gases begin with the element helium.

The halogens have strong, nasty smells. Like the alkali metals, they are very reactive. They are not usually by themselves. Instead, they are more often in compounds with other elements. Fluorine gas is pale yellow and is very dangerous to breathe. Luckily, you will not find fluorine gas floating around in nature. Fluorine is usually in safe compounds like sodium fluoride (NaF). Sodium fluoride is in toothpaste to prevent cavities.

As you have learned, table salt (NaCl) contains chlorine, a halogen. Chlorine also reacts with the element potassium. When the elements react, they form the compound potassium chloride (KCl). Potassium chloride is in medicines and plant food.

Unlike their halogen neighbors, the noble gases are not reactive. In other words, they do not combine with other elements very easily. They are usually in their pure form, not combined with any other element. One familiar noble gas is helium. Helium is a lightweight gas that gives balloons their lift. Helium is one of the most common elements in the universe. Look up at the stars! Many of them are made of helium.

Compounds made from chlorine are added to swimming pools to kill bacteria and make the water safe.

Periodic Table of Elements

																	(18)
																	4.0 **He** helium 2
(1)	(2)			**Key**		1.0 **H** hydrogen 1						(13)	(14)	(15)	(16)	(17)	
6.9 **Li** lithium 3	9.0 **Be** beryllium 4			relative atomic mass **atomic number** name atomic (proton) number								10.8 **B** boron 5	12.0 **C** carbon 6	14.0 **N** nitrogen 7	16.0 **O** oxygen 8	19.0 **F** fluorine 9	20.2 **Ne** neon 10
23.0 **Na** sodium 11	24.3 **Mg** magnesium 12	(3)	(4)	(5)	(6)	(7)	(8)	(9)	(10)	(11)	(12)	27.0 **Al** aluminium 13	28.1 **Si** silicon 14	31.0 **P** phosphorus 15	32.1 **S** sulphur 16	35.5 **Cl** chlorine 17	39.9 **Ar** argon 18
39.1 **K** potassium 19	40.1 **Ca** calcium 20	45.0 **Sc** scandium 21	47.9 **Ti** titanium 22	50.9 **V** vandium 23	52.0 **Cr** chromium 24	54.9 **Mn** manganese 25	55.8 **Fe** iron 26	58.9 **Co** cobalt 27	58.7 **Ni** nickel 28	63.5 **Cu** copper 29	65.4 **Zn** zinc 30	69.7 **Ga** gallium 31	72.6 **Ge** germanium 32	74.9 **As** arsenic 33	79.0 **Se** selenium 34	79.9 **Br** bromine 35	83.8 **Kr** krypton 36
85.5 **Rb** rubidium 37	87.6 **Sr** strontium 38	88.9 **Y** yttrium 39	91.2 **Zr** zirconium 40	92.9 **Nb** niobium 41	95.9 **Mo** molybdenum 42	98.9 **Tc** technetium 43	101.1 **Ru** ruthenium 44	102.9 **Rh** rhodium 45	106.4 **Pd** palladium 46	107.9 **Ag** silver 47	112.4 **Cd** cadmium 48	114.8 **In** indium 49	118.7 **Sn** tin 50	121.8 **Sb** antimony 51	127.6 **Te** tellurium 52	126.9 **I** iodine 53	131.3 **Xe** xenon 54
132.9 **Cs** caesium 55	137.3 **Ba** barium 56	138.9 **La *** lanthanum 57	178.5 **Hf** hafnium 72	180.9 **Ta** tantalum 73	183.9 **W** tungsten 74	186.2 **Re** rhenium 75	190.2 **Os** osmium 76	192.2 **Ir** iridium 77	195.1 **Pt** platinum 78	197.0 **Au** gold 79	200.6 **Hg** mercury 80	204.4 **Tl** thallium 81	207.2 **Pb** lead 82	209.0 **Bi** bismuth 83	210.0 **Po** polonium 84	210.0 **At** astatine 85	222.0 **Rn** radon 86
[223.0] **Fr** francium 87	[226.0] **Ra** radium 88	[227] **Ac †** actinium 89	[261] **Rf** rutherfordium 104	[262] **Db** dubnium 105	[266] **Sg** seaborgium 106	[264] **Bh** bohnium 107	[277] **Hs** hassium 108	[268] **Mt** meitnerium 109	[271] **Ds** darmstadium 110	[272] **Rg** roentgenium 111		Elements with atomic numbers 112-116 have been reported but not fully authenticad					

* 58 – 71 Lanthanides

140.1 **Ce** cerium 58	140.9 **Pr** praseodymium 59	144.2 **Nd** neodymium 60	144.9 **Pm** promethium 61	150.4 **Sm** samarium 62	152.0 **Eu** europium 63	157.3 **Gd** gadolinium 64	158.9 **Tb** terbium 65	162.5 **Dy** dysprosium 66	164.9 **Ho** holmium 67	167.3 **Er** erbium 68	168.9 **Tm** thulium 69	173.0 **Yb** ytterbium 70	175.0 **Lu** lutetium 71

† 90 – 103 Actinides

232.0 **Th** thorium 90	231.0 **Pa** protactinium 91	238.0 **U** uranium 92	237.0 **Np** neptunium 93	239.1 **Pu** plutonium 94	243.1 **Am** americium 95	247.1 **Cm** curium 96	247.1 **Bk** berkelium 97	252.1 **Cf** califomium 98	[252] **Es** einsteinium 99	[257] **Fm** fermium 100	[258] **Md** mendelevium 101	[259] **No** nobelium 102	[260] **Lr** lawrencium 103

Let There be Light

Nearly all of the noble gases are light sources in lamps. As you might guess, colorful neon lights are made from the element neon. The lights are made of glass tubes filled with neon gas. When you switch on a neon light, electricity passes through the neon inside the tube. The electricity makes the gas give off a reddish glow.

The halogens (red) are very reactive elements. The noble gases (light blue) are not reactive.

Neon, a noble gas, is used inside colorful neon lights and signs. Can you imagine these signs without their bright lights?

Compounds

Some elements, like helium, exist all by themselves in nature. More often, though, elements are part of compounds. All compounds form when elements react with other elements. It would take a chemical reaction to break the compounds apart again.

When scientists talk about compounds, they often use the compound's **chemical formula** instead of its name. A chemical formula uses the chemical symbols for each of the elements in the compound. Each molecule of water, for instance, is made of two hydrogen (H) atoms and one oxygen (O) atom. Water's chemical formula is H_2O.

Sometimes, two different compounds can contain exactly the same elements. Hydrogen peroxide (puh-**rok**-sahyd) is a clear liquid, like water. Both hydrogen peroxide and water are made of hydrogen and oxygen. But hydrogen peroxide has two atoms of oxygen, while water has just one. Hydrogen peroxide has two oxygen atoms and two hydrogen atoms. What is its chemical formula? H_2O_2 The extra oxygen atom turns hydrogen peroxide into a chemical that is used in hair bleach. Doctors also use a weaker form of hydrogen peroxide to clean cuts and scratches.

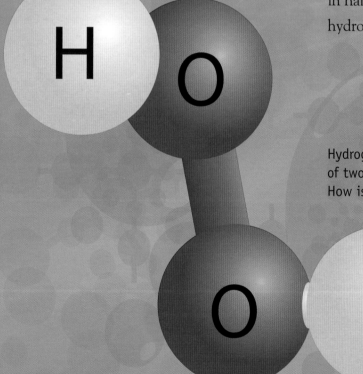

Hydrogen peroxide is a clear liquid. It is made of two hydrogen atoms and two oxygen atoms. How is it different from water?

Elements often look and behave differently when they combine into compounds. Both hydrogen and oxygen are gases when they are alone. When they are combined, they create water or hydrogen peroxide–both liquids.

Heating Up

Compounds can only be broken into elements by chemical reactions. They cannot be split by physical means such as pushing or pulling. Adding heat makes some compounds break up. Usually it takes very high temperatures to cause this chemical reaction. Water must be heated to over 2,000 degrees Celsius (3,632 Fahrenheit) before it breaks up into atoms of hydrogen and oxygen.

Some chemical compounds can be broken into their elements when they are heated to very high temperatures.

Chemical Bonds

How do the compounds and molecules stay together? Strong forces called **chemical bonds** make them "stick." Chemical bonds can hold together atoms to form a molecule. Or, chemical bonds can hold together the many molecules in a compound. You have read about table salt, a compound made from sodium and chlorine. The salt you sprinkle on your fries is not just one molecule of sodium chloride (NaCl). It is a network of many hundreds of sodium and chlorine atoms. Those atoms are all linked together to form a huge crystal. Chemical bonds hold that crystal together.

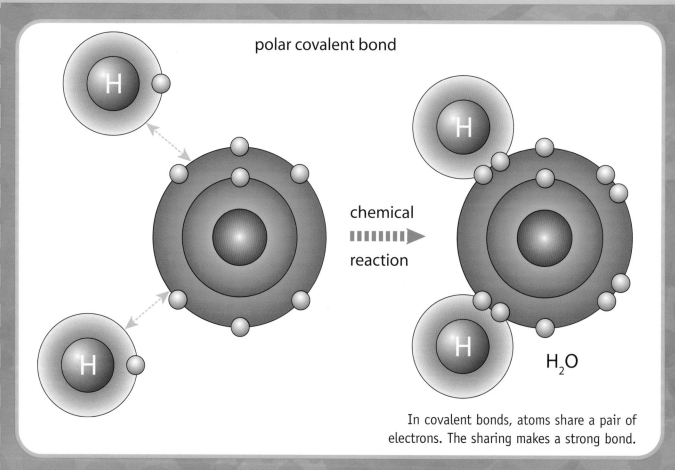

polar covalent bond

chemical ▸ reaction

H_2O

In covalent bonds, atoms share a pair of electrons. The sharing makes a strong bond.

Not all chemical bonds are alike. One of the strongest types of bonds is the **covalent bond**.

Covalent bonds form when two nonmetal elements attract one another. Hydrogen and oxygen, for example, form covalent bonds.

Covalent bonds form when two atoms share a pair of electrons. Imagine, for instance, that a hydrogen atom gets close to an oxygen atom. They are attracted to one another, so each atom donates an electron to the match. The electrons continue to circle both the hydrogen nucleus and the oxygen nucleus. By sharing their electrons, the two atoms are held together in a strong bond.

Covalent bonds are some of the strongest bonds that occur between elements and molecules. In fact, covalent bonds hold together carbon atoms in diamonds, helping to make diamonds the hardest substance known.

Hands On: Disappearing Eggshell

1. Place a whole, raw egg into a glass jar.
2. Pour vinegar into the jar to cover the egg, and screw on the lid.
3. Check on the egg over the next 24 hours.
4. What do you see? The vinegar causes a chemical reaction that breaks the bonds holding the eggshell together. The eggshell will slowly disappear.

The bonds in the eggshell don't disappear on their own. The vinegar breaks those bonds.

Waitrose
white
WINE VINEGAR
This vinegar is produced from matured white wine. Use for sauces, salad dressings and marinades.
500 ml

Another strong chemical bond is the ionic bond. Ionic bonds bind metals to nonmetals. As you just learned, covalent bonds form when atoms share electrons between them. Ionic bonds also involve electrons. In ionic bonds, though, the atoms do not share their electrons. Instead, one atom gives up its electrons. The other atom takes the electrons for itself.

Remember, electrons have a negative charge. When an atom gains an electron, it takes on a negative charge. An atom that loses an electron becomes positive. In table salt (NaCl), each sodium atom loses an electron. Sodium atoms become positively charged. Each chlorine atom takes an electron. Chlorine atoms are negatively charged.

In chemistry, opposites attract. Negative and positive atoms are attracted to one another. Think about magnets that have a positive end and a negative end. When the positive end of one magnet meets the negative end of another, they are strongly attracted to one another. The same thing happens in ionic bonds. Atoms are stuck together by the attraction between positive and negative charges.

Covalent and ionic bonds are strong forces. A weaker force called the intermolecular force holds molecules together. Picture a molecule of table salt (NaCl). The sodium and chlorine atoms are held together with ionic bonds. But each molecule of NaCl is also attracted to other molecules of NaCl. That attraction is the intermolecular force.

atoms

TRANSFER OF ELECTRON

positive ion

negative ion

ionic bond

In ionic bonds, one atom gives up its electrons. The other atom takes the electrons. This keeps the atoms bonded together.

The Hydrogen Bond

The **hydrogen bond** is a special kind of intermolecular force. It holds together molecules that contain hydrogen. In water (H_2O), the hydrogen and oxygen atoms are held together by covalent bonds. Each molecule of H_2O is also attracted to other molecules of H_2O. This attraction comes from hydrogen bonds.

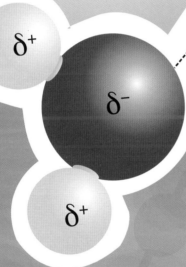

Ionic bonds hold sodium and chlorine atoms together in the compound known as table salt.

Organic Compounds

Compounds like water and table salt are only two of many millions of different chemical compounds. One group of compounds is particularly important to life. **Organic compounds** are chemical compounds that contain carbon together with at least one other element. Organic compounds make up all living things, from germs to flowers to people. Millions of organic compounds exist. In fact, there are one hundred times as many organic compounds as other kinds of compounds.

Organic chemistry is the study of organic compounds and the materials that are made from them. Many organic compounds are very useful to humans. The medicine **penicillin**, for example, is a drug used to fight infections. The active ingredient in the drug is a carbon-containing compound made by living mold. Growing mold and collecting the useful compounds can be expensive. So scientists produce **synthetic** (man-made) penicillin in laboratories. It is often cheaper for scientists to make synthetic versions of these compounds instead.

All living things are made of carbon-containing compounds called organic compounds.

Many other products besides medicines are made from organic compounds. Sweeteners used to flavor diet sodas are made from organic compounds. Carbon-containing chemicals are also used to make chemicals that kill insect pests that destroy food crops. Organic compounds are also ingredients in a common material we use every single day: plastic. In addition to all of these uses, organic compounds are important sources of energy.

Fossil Fuels

Today we get most of our energy from coal, oil, and natural gas. These materials are **fossil fuels**. Fossil fuels formed over millions of years from the remains of plants and animals. Those plants and animals were made of organic compounds. Fossil fuels contain these compounds. When we burn fossil fuels, we release energy to create electricity and fuel.

Carbon-rich fossil fuels are the source of gasoline. They take millions of years to form.

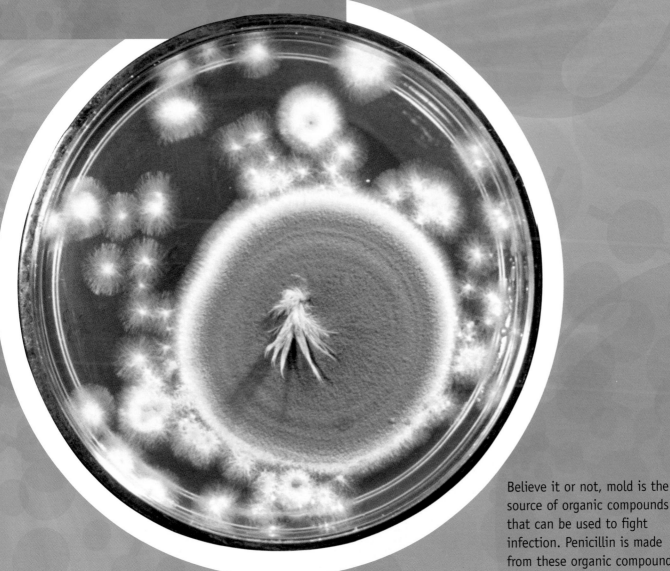

Believe it or not, mold is the source of organic compounds that can be used to fight infection. Penicillin is made from these organic compounds.

Future Chemistry

It has taken humankind thousands of years to learn about elements. Today, scientists must understand chemical compounds in order to make new medicines, for instance. Many scientists work to create new chemical compounds that do not exist in nature. Some of these compounds can cure diseases.

Chemists can also help to solve the world's energy problem. Right now, most of our energy comes from fossil fuels. Burning fossil fuels gives us energy to power our cars and light our homes. Yet burning fossil fuels also releases pollution into the air. Gases given off by fossil fuels are causing the world to slowly heat up, in a process known as **global warming**. In the future, scientists may help by finding ways to trap these gases so that they do not enter the air. Other researchers might find new fuels and energy sources that do not pollute, and do not cause the globe to heat up.

There are many problems to solve as we move into the future. Chemistry will be an important part of solving those problems. Understanding elements and compounds is the first step toward making the world a better place.

Because fossil fuels take so long to form, some chemists are trying to find ways to create fuel from plants such as corn.

Making New Elements

Scientists make a lot of things – including elements! Not all of the elements on the periodic table exist in nature. The elements with atomic numbers 93 and up were all made by scientists in the laboratory. Usually, these new elements are very unstable. Some only last a few seconds before they change into other, more stable elements.

The work of chemists can solve problems that will ensure a better future for our planet.

Chemical compounds are used in medicines. In the last decade alone, more than 160 medicines to treat rare diseases have been approved.

Glossary

actinides The radioactive elements with atomic numbers 89 through 103

alkali metals The elements lithium, sodium, potassium, rubidium, cesium, and francium

alloy Mix of metals

alkaline earth metals The elements beryllium, magnesium, calcium, strontium, barium, and radium

atom Microscopic particle that makes up all matter

atomic mass The mass of all the protons and neutrons in one atom

atomic number The number of protons in the nucleus of an atom

chemical bond Force that holds atoms and molecules together

chemical formula Code that uses chemical symbols to describe a compound

chemical symbol One- or two-letter code that represents an element

compound Substance in which atoms of two or more elements are combined

covalent bond Bond between atoms that occurs when atoms share electrons

electron Negatively charged particle that circles the nucleus of an atom

element Substance that can't be broken down into a simpler substance

flammable Able to catch fire and burn

fossil fuel Fuels such as oil, coal, and natural gas

global warming Gradual increase in the average temperature of Earth

group A vertical column of elements on the periodic table

halogens The elements fluorine, chlorine, bromine, iodine, and astatine

hydrogen bond Bonds that hold together molecules that contain hydrogen

ionic bond Bond between a positively charged atom and a negatively charged atom

isotope Two or more forms of the same element that contain equal numbers of protons but different numbers of neutrons

lanthanides The rare elements with atomic numbers 57 through 71

metal Element that is shiny, strong, and hard

metalloid Element that has some, but not all, properties of metals

mineral Natural compounds formed through Earth's actions

molecule Group of atoms held together in a larger particle

neutron Uncharged particle in the nucleus of an atom

noble gases The elements helium, neon, argon, krypton, xenon, and radon

nucleus The core of an atom, which contains neutrons and protons

ore Mixture of rocks that contains metals or minerals, such as gold

organic compound Chemical compound that contains carbon and at least one other element

penicillin Infection-fighting medicine made from organic compounds in mold

periodic table A chart of the elements according to their atomic numbers

proton Positively charged particle in the nucleus of an atom

radiation Energy given off by radioactive elements

radioactive Elements that are unstable and lose their atomic particles over time

reactive Elements that react strongly with water or other elements

synthetic Man-made

transition elements The metals in the center of the periodic table

Index

Web Finder

http://www.chem4kids.com/files/elem_intro.html

http://education.jlab.org/atomtour/

http://www.rsc.org/chemsoc/visualelements/pages/periodic_table.html

http://www.elements-of-life.org/eol_index_flash.html

http://www.sciencenewsforkids.org/articles/20080116/Note2.asp

http://www.pbs.org/wgbh/nova/kaboom/elemental/

http://www.webelements.com

Printed in the U.S.A.